© Aladdin Books Ltd 1990

Design   David West
                    Children's Book Design
Editor   Steve Parker
Photo researcher   Cecilia Weston-Baker
Consultant   Dr. Michael Gossop

First published in the   The publishers would like to
United States in 1990 by   acknowledge that the photographs
Franklin Watts   reproduced within this book have
387 Park Avenue South   been posed by models or have
New York NY 10016   been obtained from photographic
                                agencies
Printed in Belgium

Library of Congress Cataloging-in-Publication Data

Algeo, Philippa.
        Acid and hallucinogens / Philippa Algeo.
            p.   cm. -- (Understanding drugs)
        Summary: Describes LSD and other hallucinogenic drugs, their
    effects on the nervous system, and their long-term consequences.
        ISBN 0-531-10932-1
        1. LSD (Drug)--Physiological effect--Juvenile literature.
    2. Hallucinogenic drugs--Physiological effect--Juvenile literature.
    3. Neuropharmacology--Juvenile literature. [1. LSD (Drug)
    2. Hallucinogenic drugs. 3. Drugs. 4. Drug abuse.] I. Title.
    II. Series.
    RM666.L88A48   1990
    615'.7883--dc20   89-70497   CIP   AC

Contents

UNDERSTANDING DRUGS

ACID AND HALLUCINOGENS

Philippa Algeo

FRANKLIN WATTS

London · New York · Toronto · Sydney

INTRODUCTION

In the 1960s young people, especially students, found a "new" drug. First in the United States and then in Britain, people began to take LSD, or "acid." It was the "in" thing to do and the drug was an important part of the youth culture of the time. The LSD "guru," American psychologist Timothy Leary, advised everyone to: "Tune in, turn on and drop out." At this time the word "psychedelic" came into common use, not only to describe the mind-altering effects of the drug, but to describe the music and art that was created by users.

"Flower power" was the term used to describe the way these young people thought about life and how to live – essentially peacefully and lovingly, at one with nature. So they would take LSD, smoke marijuana (cannabis), and listen to LSD-inspired rock music. Together they would slide away from reality into philosophical, almost religious experiences. They would see objects differently, colors more brightly, and be enveloped by the music. Their senses would fuse and they would hallucinate – hear images, see sounds.

Other hallucinogenic substances sometimes used illicitly included mescaline, from the peyote cactus, psilocybin and psilocin from certain mushrooms, and more recently PCP (phencyclidine or "angel dust") and the MDA group of drugs, particularly MDMA or "ecstasy." Marijuana, used in large enough quantities, can also produce mind-altering effects.

The face of flower power: hippies gather for a concert in the 60s.

The demand for LSD dropped during the 1970s, due to fear of its dangerous effects, the legal ban on its manufacture, sale and consumption, and the successful police efforts to track down the manufacturers and dealers, particularly "Operation Julie" in the United Kingdom in 1977.

But once again LSD use is on the increase. The scene surrounding the drug no longer has a religious, intellectual or creative aura. It is just one of many banned substances taken for its hallucinogenic effects, its power to transform, and its relatively low cost. But what is the truth about the drug? What is it like? What can it do?

Information was gathered when the drug was first discovered and was being used to treat people with psychological illnesses. It was also investigated for its potential use in chemical warfare. But much of that information is unreliable because the people who were researching it had something to gain from its general acceptance. The manufacturers stood to gain financially; the United States, involved in the Korean war, was interested in its potential as a weapon. Psychiatrists hoped it might hold the key to treatment of mental illness such as schizophrenia; and the leaders of the hippy revolution, who wanted to convince people of its value in creating a world based on "flower power" ideals, stood to gain personally.

Because it is such a dangerous chemical, and because it is strictly illegal to make, sell and use it, little new research has gone on into the effects of LSD. Virtually no medical use is made of LSD now. Up-to-date information comes from people who are receiving treatment for illegal drug-taking.

WHY DO PEOPLE TAKE ACID?

I was told I would have a great time... it didn't work out like that.

"Acid" is the best known of the common names for LSD. There are many "street" names for the drug including blotter acid, purple haze, sugar cubes, sunshine, microdots, tabs, or Lucy in the sky with diamonds. These names refer to the form in which acid is available or to songs associated with it.

Lysergic acid diethylamide is the full name given to this powerful substance. It is prepared from ergot, a fungus found growing on rye and other wild grasses. In medieval times, European communities who made bread from rye would occasionally suffer a terrible sickness called St. Anthony's Fire. Symptoms of sufferers included hallucinations, convulsions and gangrene (blackening and death of soft tissue due to loss of blood supply). They would go on pilgrimages to St. Anthony's Shrine to pray for the relief of their sickness, leaving their ergot-infected rye bread at home. All but the gangrene symptoms would pass.

What are hallucinations?

One of the effects LSD can cause is illusion or hallucination, when the user sees objects either differently or sees things that don't exist. With LSD, users are generally aware that it is the drug that is creating the hallucinations. When the user fails to have this awareness (sometimes after taking a large dose), then the hallucinations become "real" – there is no consciousness of the imagination at work and this can lead to a "bad trip." Prepared for sale to illegal drug users, LSD is usually a white powder. The acid itself is added to other

Psychologist Timothy Leary, LSD "guru."

powdered substances and formed into tablets or put into capsules. Or it may be in a clear liquid. This is then added to sugar cubes or absorbed onto paper – stamp-like pieces of paper with colored pictures of cartoon or movie characters like ET or the Pink Panther. Sometimes it is on blotting paper or in gelatin. All of these are chewed or swallowed, and you absorb the drug through the normal digestive processes. Very rarely LSD is injected or inhaled.

> **❝❝ I thought I was being conned – I could hardly see the stuff. First-time-user, Chicago. ❞❞**

LSD is incredibly potent. A minute amount can send you sky high. A microgram is one millionth of a gram. If you took 10 micrograms of LSD you would feel a bit drunk. A full-blown "trip" can result from taking just 50 micrograms. The usual dose is between 100 and 150 micrograms.

What happens after you take LSD?
About half an hour after the user consumes LSD orally (it has a quicker effect when injected) the intoxication takes effect. The trip will intensify and be at its height between two and six hours after taking the drug. The effects then gradually wear off until the user feels fairly normal after about 12 hours. But it is impossible to give exact information on duration and intensity of a trip since this depends on the dose taken and the state of mind of the user.

The drug has an ability to provoke sensations of euphoria and joy, and a dreamlike experience. But it sometimes creates deep feelings of unhappiness instead. Colors seem brighter and more intense. Sounds distort, expand, and envelop. Sometimes sounds and colors become confused, as if you could hear color or see sound.

> **❝❝ I was told I would have a great time...it didn't work out like that.** Convicted acid user, aged 17. **❞❞**

You may feel as if somehow you are outside your own body, observing it and your drug-induced experience. Objects, your own body, shapes, sizes and spaces distort, and you lose your ability to judge size, distance and space. You lose your ability to coordinate your body movements. Like some of the hippy generation you may feel an almost religious experience, and have what you feel at the time to be great insights into the human condition.

The physical effects of taking LSD vary. You may tremble and feel weak. You may feel dizzy, your heart may pound. You might find yourself panting. Your head can ache, and you can have feelings of numbness. The pupils in your eyes will dilate and you will find it difficult to focus. Sometimes people vomit. You may feel hot, sweaty and shivery.

> **❝❝ It's not what you take, it's the person that takes it. ❞❞**

It is impossible to say exactly what the experience will be like mentally for any individual. And this is the great danger of LSD. *It is totally unpredictable.*

If you are a well balanced person (not given to feelings of

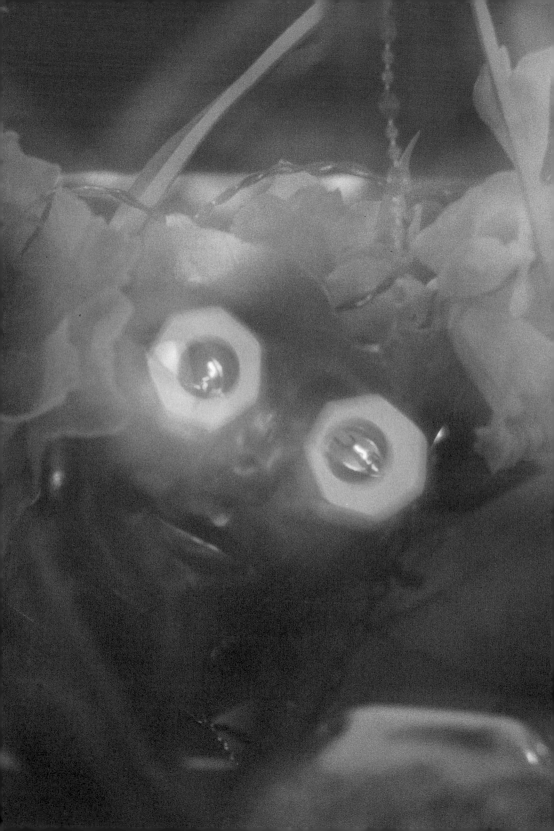

depression or anxiety), if you are in a safe and comfortable place, with people who know you, know what you are doing, and know how to deal with a person experiencing a "bad trip," if you know you are not taking a dangerously high dose (still a minute amount), then you *might* not suffer too much. But sometimes people who have taken LSD and had several good trips suddenly and for no foreseeable reason have a terrifying experience. A trip that starts out well can change, confusion and anxiety can crowd in.

In spite of the little that is known about LSD some things are clear. If you are anxious or depressed you will feel worse. It is thought that LSD can bring about mental illness in those already predisposed to psychotic conditions. Severely depressed people risk feeling the desire to commit suicide when under the influence of LSD.

The "bad trip"

When people trip and feel they are losing control of their minds they can become very frightened. Psychologists call it panic – that feeling of knowing something terrible is happening and being unable to do anything about it. This develops into the "bad trip," the experience gone wrong, when "mind-blowing" fear develops. The user may recall this fear without conscious prompting long after the event.

Flashbacks

If you are alone or with inexperienced people, and you find

Taking LSD can become a nightmare experience.

your mind wandering in an apparently uncontrollable way, you could have feelings of intense panic. These feelings can sometimes return when you have not taken the drug, and this is called a "flashback." For no particular reason you relive bad moments of a trip when you least expect it. This can happen weeks, even months, after taking LSD.

Whoever is with you should know that reassurance and calm are essential for the person having a bad experience with LSD. Reassurance means telling the sufferer that their feelings are a result of the drug they have taken, that these feelings are not real and will pass very soon.

If you have a friend experiencing a bad trip, you must try to calm them by talking in a low and gentle voice. Remind them that they are only having a bad trip and that this will soon stop and that they are safe and will not be left alone. Don't leave the sufferer alone unless it is essential to get extra help. It will take time to wear off, maybe hours. Turn anyone who seems unconscious onto their right side. If they vomit make sure they do not choke by clearing the air passages. Get emergency medical help.

A danger to yourself and others
Under LSD you will be unable to judge distance or shapes, your objective judgment will be impaired, and you could be a danger to yourself and to others. Driving a car or using any potentially dangerous machinery could be fatal.

People undergoing a trip can behave irrationally and

Fear can develop as shapes blur and senses merge.

unpredictably and this is what sensation-seeking news-papers have reported. It may be that you feel you can fly – hopefully no one will let you try.

Regular use

You cannot keep taking LSD day after day. It loses its effect after about three or four days. In other words your body becomes tolerant of it, and will not respond. A user has to stop taking it for a few days or even a couple of weeks before trying again.

Because of this it is said that LSD does not create physical dependence or addiction. But in some cases users do want it again, in spite of bad trips, flashbacks, and accidents. This is a kind of psychological dependence – your body doesn't crave the drug, but psychologically the user wants more.

> **❝ I was persuaded to try it the first time because I was told I could not become addicted...but I do want it again. Small-time dealer, Seattle. ❞**

Long-term effects

While it is said that LSD does not create physical dependence, there are effects, some proved and some only suspected, that can be attributed to taking LSD.

People who, although previously unsuspected, are prone to mental illnesses, particularly schizophrenia, can become mentally ill. This condition may wear off if they are lucky. The

LSD is unpredictable: for many, the experience turns sour.

less fortunate face a lifetime of needing treatment from psychiatrists. Flashbacks can recur indefinitely, leaving the sufferer depressed and bewildered, reexperiencing a bad trip or a bad moment from a trip.

Since behavior during a trip can be unpredictable and unreasonable, injuries sustained at that time can cause death or long-term physical damage.

Although it is not clear what constitutes an overdose of LSD, few deaths have been recorded as a result of it.

Frequent users of LSD sometimes suffer from problems of motivation. They have no enthusiasm or drive, and often just sit around doing nothing, waiting for the next time they can escape into an unreal, drug-created world. Heavy marijuana users can also find themselves in this situation.

LSD AND THE HIPPY DREAM

❝ *My mom talks about 'flower power'... it all sounds a little silly to me.* ❞

When LSD was first discovered, scientists believed that a powerful and helpful drug had been found. Albert Hofmann was a research scientist working for a Swiss chemical company, Sandoz. In 1938 he isolated LSD but was unable to do any further work with it. However, in 1943 he accidentally ingested some of this new substance. He had to go home from work and lie down, and he wrote about what we now know to be the first LSD trip. He said he felt intoxicated, like being drunk. He was restless, dizzy. He felt in a dream-like state, his imagination stimulated. He saw an "uninterrupted stream of fantastic pictures, extraordinary shapes with intense kaleidoscopic play of colors." After a few hours, his mind returned to normal and he felt fine.

The Swiss company supplied large amounts of LSD to American researchers, and to the Central Intelligence Agency (CIA). Psychiatrists began to use the drug to treat people with mental illnesses, particularly schizophrenia, where patients feel a disconnection between themselves and their thoughts and actions.

The CIA tried to find a way of developing LSD for use in chemical warfare. They thought that use of the drug on their enemies might enable them to subdue a whole mass of people and brainwash them into submission. It was known to be extremely potent – a minute dose of 50 millionths of a gram (five micrograms) could bring about mind-altering effects. Because such a large amount of the substance existed, and because it was easy to make, it found its way

Swiss chemist Albert Hofmann, the "father of LSD."

through the researchers and lecturers in American universities to students and they used it along with marijuana as a "recreational drug."

❝ *My mom talks about 'flower power' and says she was a 'hippy'...it all sounds a little silly to me.* **College student from Portland.** ❞

When LSD was most popular – during the 1960s and early 70s – it was tied in with the way young people were thinking, the music they liked to listen to, and modern or "pop" art. Peace, love and the natural world were seen to be the most

Dangerous doses: various forms of LSD.

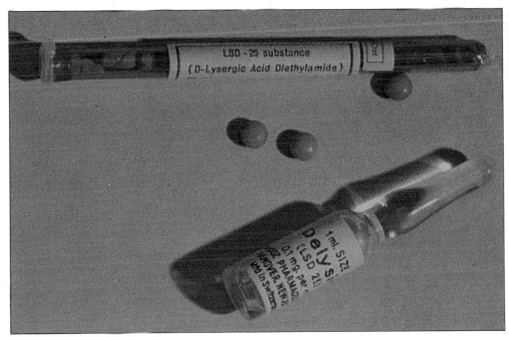

LSD was first researched as a possible chemical weapon.

important elements of life. War, conflict and commercialism were seen to be characteristics of older people, and were heavily criticized by the young. They were convinced that if people could love each other war would disappear and life would be beautiful. Feelings of love and goodwill could, they thought, be created by taking LSD and marijuana.

> **❝❝ *We thought we were changing the world – the music and drugs were part of it.* Ex-hippy, Swindon, England. ❞❞**

The hippy revolution was not basically weird or immoral – it sprang from a desire for peace and love. It was a kind of new religion – the old religions were too closely involved with the society that the young people were rejecting. Young people today have similar feelings of rejection but with added hopelessness, and drug taking is very much tied in with this.

> **❝❝ *Some 60s music is really strange..I can't under- stand the words sometimes.* Scottish teenager. ❞❞**

Popular music had undergone a revolution. Rock music of the 1950s developed and by the time groups like the Beatles, the Rolling Stones, Frank Zappa, the Jimi Hendrix Experience, Pink Floyd, the Grateful Dead, and Jefferson Airplane were popular, LSD and similar drugs were in

The music of Jimi Hendrix was popular during the hippy era.

common use. The music was influenced by the drugs, as musicians tried to recreate sounds they heard when listening to music while tripping.

Modern art, too, was influenced. LSD users saw colors more brightly, images were distorted. Artists experimented with their materials to try to recreate what they saw while using LSD.

THE DREAM THAT WON'T GO AWAY

❝ I wanted to hear colors, see sounds, feel high... but I was just scared stiff. ❞

Where do drugs like acid come from now?

Because LSD is easily and cheaply manufactured there is no way of knowing exactly where it comes from. In the United Kingdom for example, seizures of the chemical by police are fairly widespread throughout the country. Its use is limited, but gradually increasing. It is fairly cheap – about $5.00 a tab of about 50 micrograms. It is often available through dealers who handle other drugs, marijuana in particular, as the two drugs have historically been connected, even taken at the same time.

> ❝❝ *At a party, I was offered a Pink Panther stamp and was told it was LSD.* **Hairdresser, aged 20.** ❝❝

First contact with any drug is likely to be through a friend, and so the network establishes itself. Parties and nightclubs are typically events where drugs are found and passed.

> ❝❝ *You can never believe what you are being told about a dose by anyone – even your best friend – because the source of information is unreliable.* **Health worker, Birmingham.** ❝❝

It is very difficult to know what exactly is being passed, particularly with LSD and similar substances. The results of tests done on LSD that has been seized by police show that about two thirds of the samples were pure. That means that

Content unknown: LSD capsules change hands.

about one third was either some other substance or that the LSD had been mixed with something else, like methedrine, amphetamine or strychnine – poison!

Who takes hallucinogenic drugs?

Surveys have shown that about 1 percent of the British population has at some time used acid. In the United States the informed estimate of the numbers of people who have ever used LSD is around 4.5 percent of adults and 6 percent of youth. Because these drugs are illegal, it is difficult to obtain accurate figures. In the 60s and 70s people who wanted to take these drugs were typically students. Today it seems that these drugs do not have the same intellectual pretensions and use is more evenly spread.

The manufacturers and dealers

Recreational drug users are at the mercy of dealers. The dealers and manufacturers are not known for their honesty. Their whole business is based on being on the wrong side of the law and making as much money as possible. The equipment and skills used in illegally making LSD and selling it are not very sophisticated. When such small amounts are involved, even a moderate dose can cause frightening and damaging effects.

You never know where or when you will be offered drugs, or by whom. It might be your best friend. It is unlikely to be a total stranger. It might be at a party, a nightclub, or just

Drugs may be offered at an "acid house" party.

between friends at home. Newspapers have built up the idea that anyone and everyone who goes to a so-called "acid house party" will be "out of their minds" on LSD.

❝❝ Newspapers give young people a bad name. You would think that every party is just an excuse for taking drugs. Keen party-goer, Aberdeen. ❞❞

That is not particularly true. People go to enjoy themselves at an event with loud music, bright lights and dancing, held in a secret venue not known to the police before it has all happened. Probably there will be drugs, although these

The smiling face of "acid house" may mask drug dealing.

Rock music may still be influenced by the drug culture today.

events are not generally associated with heavy alcohol use. The drugs might be anything from marijuana to crack.

❝ *I wanted to hear colors, see sounds, feel high... but I was just scared stiff.* Manual laborer, London. ❞

At a party a friend will often try to involve other friends that can be trusted, and will usually offer a drug they have already tried themselves. Once involved in the drug scene you might be offered any number of different substances.

The greatest danger of all is taking a "cocktail" of drugs – smoking marijuana at the same time as taking LSD and amphetamines, for example.

"MAGIC" MUSHROOMS ?

❝ Consuming the wrong species could be fatal. ❞

Many agencies can help "kick the habit."

Wanting help and a strong desire to get rid of the hold that drugs have over the user are the main essentials to getting help.

There are numerous sources of help, but the hard work has to be done. Determination will always receive support from others, if the user knows where to find it.

Parents

Although there will always be people who feel that they cannot go to their parents for help (because they feel their parents would not understand or would be very unhappy), never count them out.

Because LSD and marijuana have been around since the

early 60s, parents know about them and may even have used them – although they are unlikely to confess this to their children.

The instant reaction may be anger, shouting, fear, sorrow, tears – probably all of these things. But parents will, in most cases, want to help. Give them time to overcome the instant reaction, then tell them you want their help. If they shout, it is because they are very upset; they probably feel they have failed you.

Give them time.

Outside agencies

There are many outside agencies that can help. Into this category come doctors and hospitals, family counseling agencies, citizens' advice bureaus, and specialist drug advisory services.

Doctors

Whatever the nature and seriousness of your involvement, your family doctor can help. Your mental and physical health are his or her primary concern and you should receive a sympathetic and positive consultation. Your doctor is aware of the drugs and their effects, and also knows the specialist agencies who can support and advise you.

Emergency

If you are with anyone undergoing a bad trip, or who has suffered personal injury as a result of taking a drug, seems to be comatose (unconscious), or is having a convulsion, get help. Telephone a doctor (without additional panic on your part), or parents or other helpful persons. Never leave the person alone.

❝❝ *My friend was with me ...he got help...*Former acid user from a small town in the Mid-West. ❞❞

Beyond any first aid treatment you know, such as turning the person onto their right side, you need professional assistance. In an emergency call 911.

Family advice agencies

There are voluntary and statutory agencies who will help in a nonemergency situation, whether this means getting help for yourself or for a friend. These agencies have a databank of sources of specialist advice and treatment.

Drug advice services

These bodies are government funded and have specially trained people employed to help drug abusers and their families. This does not mean that they are wolves in sheep's clothing. Their primary role is to help people with a drug problem. Addresses and telephone numbers are at the back of this book. If the number is not local to you, call them anyway and you will be referred to a more local office.

Legal help

There are organizations who offer legal help if you get "busted" (arrested) for drug offenses. Their names, addresses and telephone numbers appear at the back of this book.

You are your first source of help. Find the determination and make the first step in the right direction and you should find all the help that you need.

FACTFILE

LSD stands for Lysergic acid diethylamide. It was first discovered in 1938 by Albert Hofmann, a chemist working in the natural products section of the Swiss firm Sandoz Pharmaceuticals. While carrying out further work on the drug in 1943, Hofmann experienced the first LSD "trip."

LSD is derived from the ergot fungus that is found growing on rye and other wild grasses.

Research on the effective use of the drug was carried out during the 50s and early 60s, until its recreational use became so widespread that in 1966 it was limited by law in both the United States and Britain. In 1971 the United Nations placed LSD on a list of severely restricted drugs in the regulations called Psychotropic Substances 1971. In Britain the drug is severely limited as a Class A substance under the Misuse of Drugs Act 1971. Mescaline, psilocybin, and MDA are similarly covered in law. Marijuana is a Class B drug under the same law.

LSD is very potent. 50 millionths of a gram (50 micrograms) can have a powerful effect. The normal dose is about 100-150 micrograms. It appears on the market commonly absorbed onto colored paper. These stamp-like papers generally have cartoon characters printed on them, such as ET or Pink Panther. It may also be found in tablet or capsule form, or in gelatin wafers. As a transparent liquid it can be absorbed onto sugar cubes or blotting paper. Rarely, it is injected or inhaled.

The drug no longer has a mainly student following. It is found, as other drugs are, in nightclubs and at parties.

Hallucinogens are drugs that alter perception, that is they can cause the user to see objects, see colors, or hear sounds differently; in fact the senses can merge. But these are pseudo-hallucinations. Seeing things that are not there is a true hallucination. This occurs rarely with LSD and similar drugs and is usually associated with a high dose or some other factor, such as a predis-position to mental illness in the user.

Mescaline is derived from the peyote cactus. It is found in the form of white powder.

Psilocybin and psilocin are found naturally in hallucinogenic mushrooms. The main species are *Psilocybe semilanceata* or Liberty Cap and some *Paneolus* species. In the United States the main species is *Psilocybe mexicana*. There are other mushrooms that closely resemble these species that are poisonous. Fly Agaric *Amanita muscaria* is poisonous. It also has hallucinogenic properties.

Marijuana, a mild hallucinogen, is produced from a hemp plant and is smoked, either in a cigarette or pipe. Its use is widespread. It is found either as a tobacco, resin or oil.

The MDA group of compounds combine the effects of amphetamine and hallucinogen. MDMA, street name "ecstasy," is prevalent at the moment. It is usually found in tablet form. Levels of purity in samples seized, however, throw doubts on the truth of what users are told, as many contain other compounds and often LSD, which is cheaper.

DRUG PROFILE: LSD

Common names LSD, Acid.

Other names Big D, Blotter, California sunshine, Dot, Electric Kool Aid, Lucy in the sky with diamonds, Microdots, Paper acid, Paper mushrooms, Peace, Purple haze, Sugar, Sugar cubes.

Made from Ergot fungus or chemically manufactured.

Drug type Hallucinogen

Main actions Increased sensory awareness; distortions of sight, sound, and other senses; mixing of senses, for example sight and sound; feelings of disassociation; mystical insights. Occasionally deep feelings of anxiety mounting to panic. Restlessness or sleepiness. Physical effects include dilation of pupils, increased heart rate and blood pressure, shivering and sweating; poor coordination.

Addictiveness LSD is not physically addictive. The body quickly becomes tolerant. Use has to cease for up to two weeks before sensitivity to the drug returns. Psychological need may be created.

Risks LSD is completely unpredictable, because the state of mind, health and expectations of users greatly affect a trip. Suicide under the influence of LSD is known. Because tolerance is quickly built up there is little evidence of long-term physical damage. Few known cases of overdose.

Main producers There are manufacturers in most countries where it is taken.

Number of users This seems to have remained a fairly constant 1% of the population (about 650,000 in Britain) as an "ever-used" figure. Since 1979 the figures for seizures of LSD by the police and numbers of people found guilty under the M.D.A. have gradually increased.

Example of cost About $5.00 for 50 micrograms.

Legal status LSD is a Class A drug controlled under the Misuse of Drugs Act. It is illegal to manufacture, supply or possess LSD, or allow your premises to be used for manufacturing or supplying the drug.

Examples of penalties You could go to prison for up to seven years for possessing LSD. More serious offenses of trading attract heavy sentences of up to lifetime imprisonment.

SOURCES OF HELP

Here are addresses and telephone numbers of organizations that may be able to provide further information on LSD, its effects, health risks and legal status.

National Hotlines
National Institute on Drug Abuse Treatment Referral
1 (800) 622-HELP
Weekdays: 9:00 am – 3:00 am, weekends: 12 noon – 3:00 am.
Counselors are on hand if you need someone to talk to; also call for referrals in your area or if you have a question about drugs, drug treatment, health or legal problems.

New York State Division of Substance Abuse
1 (800) 522-5353
Over-the-telephone crisis intervention by experienced counselors. Also call for referrals or advice.

National Federation of Parents for Drug Free Youth
1 (800) 554-KIDS
Educational organization offering informational pamphlets, books and videos.

National Association for Drug Abuse
355 Lexington Avenue
New York, N.Y. 10017
(212) 986-1170
Conducts a drug prevention program and provides family counseling.

National Association of State Boards of Education
P.O. Box 1176
Alexandria, VA 22313
(703) 684-4000
Booklet available.

National Clearinghouse for Drug Abuse Information
P.O. Box 2305
Rockville, MD 20850
Provides information on a variety of drugs.

National Self Help Clearinghouse
33 West 42nd Street
New York, N.Y. 10036
(212) 840-1259
Provides information on self-help rehabilitation organizations and clearinghouses throughout the country.

Addiction Research Foundation
33 Russell Street
Toronto, Ontario MSS 231
(416) 595-6100
Provides general reference service free to Ontario residents.

Alcohol and Drug Problems Association of North America
444 N. Capitol Street
Suite 181
Washington, D.C. 20001
(202) 737-4340
Answers inquiries, makes referrals.

Alcohol, Drug Abuse and Mental Health Administration
Public Health Service
Department of Health and Human Services
Parklawn Building
Room 12C-15
5600 Fishers Lane
Rockville, MD 20857
(301) 443-3783
Handles inquiries, fills requests for publications.

WHAT THE WORDS MEAN

Acid Lysergic acid diethylamide

Addictive causing physical need for the drug in order for the user to stay "normal" and stave off the physical and mental effects of withdrawal

Amphetamines drugs that stimulate the central nervous system

Bad trip an unpleasant effect of taking LSD. The user, often anxious before taking the drug, finds his thoughts and emotions are out of control. The best help he can have is calm reassurance that this is only the effect of the drug and it will pass

Busted arrested by the police

Buzz the effects of a drug

Dependence the need to keep taking a drug regularly, either for its effects on the body (to keep away withdrawal symptoms, for instance) or for its effects on the mind

DMT dimethyltriptamine an hallucinogenic drug similar to LSD

Drop acid take LSD

Drug any chemical or other substance that changes the body's functions (including the way the person's mind works, his behavior, etc.)

Drug abuse non-medical drug use with harmful effects, on the abuser and possibly on others

Drug misuse using drugs in a way which people in general would see as not sensible, or not acceptable, and possibly harmful

Flashback reliving a bad moment from a trip some time after the effects of the drug have worn off

Hallucination being aware, through one or other of the body's senses, of someone or something that is not there at all. Quasi-hallucinations, experienced during a "normal" LSD trip, occur when the drug user is aware of the fact that it is the workings of the drug that is creating the images, sounds, etc.

Microgram one millionth of a gram; a minute, barely visible amount

Psilocybin, psilocin drugs from Psilocybe mushrooms that have hallucinogenic effect

Psychedelic a term brought into common use in the 1960s as a means of describing the mind-altering effects of LSD; it also described the music and art produced by users of LSD

Psychoactive drug a drug that has mind-altering effects

Schizophrenia a form of mental illness where the sufferer loses control of his thoughts

Speed amphetamine

Stoned under the influence of drugs

Synesthesia a merging of the senses giving the impression that images can be heard, sounds can be seen, etc.

Tolerance the body's ability to cope with the effects of the drug and maintain normal functioning

Toxic poisonous; harmful to the body

Trip psychological effects of LSD

INDEX

Photographic Credits:
Cover and pages 12, 17, 29, 39, 49 and 51: Roger Vlitos; pages 4, 41 and 45: Topham Picture Library; page 7: Lowe/Network Photographers; page 9: Frank Spooner Agency; pages 15, 35, 37 and 43: Robert Harding Library; pages 19, 27 and 53: Magnum Photos; page 20: Popperfoto; pages 22, 25, 31 and 47: Rex Features; page 32: Network Photographers; page 33: David Browne; page 55: Marie-Helene Bradley.